Croydon Airport
The Peaceful Years

Lufthansa's Focke-Wulf Condor D-AETA *Westfalen*, the second prototype, lands over the Aer Lingus D.H.86B EI-ABK in 1938. The latter was originally G-ADVJ of Blackpool & West Coast Air Services before sale to Aer Lingus in September 1936. Restored to the British register in October 1946, it was last reported derelict at Bahrain in 1952.

Croydon Airport
The Peaceful Years

Mike Hooks

TEMPUS

The height of the Imperial Airways hangar at Croydon is evident here, with Short L-17 G-ACJJ undergoing maintenance with a pair of D.H.86s – G-AEAP *Demeter* was impressed in Egypt as HK843 in October 1941, but was burnt out at Pachino, Sicily, on 23 July 1943 while G-ACJJ was wrecked in a gale on 14 September 1940 at Drem, Scotland.

First published 2002
Copyright © Mike Hooks, 2002

Tempus Publishing Limited
The Mill, Brimscombe Port,
Stroud, Gloucestershire, GL5 2QG
www.tempus-publishing.com

ISBN 0 7524 2758 X

TYPESETTING AND ORIGINATION BY
Tempus Publishing Limited
PRINTED IN GREAT BRITAIN BY
Midway Colour Print, Wiltshire

Contents

An interesting apron scene showing Alpar's Koolhoven FK.50 HB-AMA, Olley Air Service Dragon Rapide G-AGSI and Consul G-AHFS. While no date is given, it can be deduced as between summer 1947 and summer 1949 by one of the Ansons in the background, G-AHIE, only current around that period.

Passengers embarking on British Airways Lockheed Electra G-AFEB with another alongside, L-17 G-ACJJ and KLM DC-2 PH-AKT. British Airways operated seven Electras with a two-man crew and seating for ten passengers. 'FEB was impressed as W9104 with No.24 Squadron but was written off in October 1941. The DC-2 was captured by the Luftwaffe when Holland was over-run in May 1940 and, coded NA+LA, became the personal aircraft of General Christensen, the German military commander of the Netherlands.

Armstrong Whitworth Argosy II G-AAEJ was the last of seven Argosies operated by Imperial Airways, receiving its C of A in August 1929. It was later christened *City of Coventry*. Powered by three 420hp Armstrong Siddeley Jaguar engines, it could carry twenty-eight passengers on European routes. It was dismantled at Croydon in 1935; note the complex exhaust systems!

Introduction

In 1997 the Chalford Publishing Company commissioned me to produce a book in their Archive Photographs series entitled *Croydon Airport*. This briefly covered the airport's life from 1915 to its closure in 1959, using my own photographs, and with considerable help from members of the Croydon Airport Society, of which I have been a member for some years. The few wartime photographs available were included in that volume and no more have been discovered for this one, hence the title chosen.

The London Borough of Sutton Libraries and Arts Services produced three excellent volumes on the airport's history – *The First Croydon Airport 1915-1928*, *The Great Days 1928-1939* and *Croydon Airport and the Battle of Britain 1939-1940* – and the CAS has a final volume in preparation. These books are an admirable history of the airport, its personalities and the aircraft which passed through.

My own offerings do not seek to cover that type of detail, but since the 1997 book (ISBN 0-7524-0744-9), which was reprinted in 2001 by the same company, now renamed Tempus, many additional photographs have become available from the CAS archives, thanks to members' responses to appeals.

This book concentrates on the wide variety of aircraft types which visited the airport. I make no apology for the poor quality of some of the photographs, which may be up to eighty years old, but are of interest. The colour pages depicting aircraft in the final years of the airport's life have, for production reasons, had to be placed in the centre of the book; some were used in monochrome in the previous book.

Photographs are roughly in chronological order – so for instance all Dakotas are not together – and dates are given where known. Most of my own photographs I have been able to date by reference to my log books which started in 1946, so being a spotter has been – and still is – of great value!

A page from Captain 'Jerry' Shaw's log book – he was the pilot of the first London-Amsterdam service on 17 May 1920 in Airco D.H.16 G-EALU with two passengers and goods. It took 135 minutes, was flown at 300ft and the weather was very bad. Returning the next day took 215 minutes at 250ft with three passengers – uncomfortable journeys! Other flights on this page involved tests and joy rides – note the forced landing at Lympne on 14 June.

Acknowledgements

I am greatly indebted to the Croydon Airport Society for permission to use photographs from their archives and in particular would like to record the considerable help given by Peter Skinner in the search for unusual photographs.

The following are contributors whose names have been identified, along with the page number and position of their photographs:

C. Barnes: p.94 top, p.96 bottom, p.103 top, p.104 bottom, p.105 bottom, p.106 top & bottom, p.107 bottom, p.108 bottom, p.110 bottom, p.112 bottom, p.113 top, p.114 top, p.115 top, p.117 top & bottom, p.118 top, p.119 top & bottom, p.120 centre & bottom; P. Barrington: p.81 bottom, p.84 bottom, p.86 bottom; L.R. Burness: p.14 top, p.16 centre & bottom, p.38 top & centre, p.40 top; M. Clark: p.72 bottom; E. Crawforth: p.100 top; C. Cruddas: p.11 top; A.W. Eagle: p.52 top; P. Lintott via N. Owen: p.65 bottom, p.66 top, p.68 bottom, p.69 bottom, p.70 top & bottom, p.73 bottom; R. Nicholls: p.100 bottom; F. Olin via P. Izard; p.64 bottom; Mrs R. Quirk via T. Barnes: p.10 top, p.21 top, p.22 top, p.26 bottom, p.27 bottom, p.28 top & bottom, p.40 bottom; D. Schofield: p.77 bottom, p.78 bottom, p.82 top & bottom, p.83 top & bottom, p.85 top, p.86 top, p.91 centre & bottom, p.116 bottom; P. Skinner: final nine photographs in colour section; B.N. Stainer: p.19 bottom, p.21 top, p.33 top, p.39 top; P.T. Staley: p.93 bottom, p.97 bottom, p.98 top; H. Stilwell via H. Trudd: p.57 top.

I am also grateful to the editor of *Aeroplane* for permission to use some prints from their archives; apologies for any credits which I have missed.

If you have found this book interesting, you may wish to join the Croydon Airport Society which holds monthly meetings in the airport terminal booking hall. Membership details may be obtained from Mrs Margaret White, 38 Long Walk, Tattenham Corner, Epsom, Surrey KT18 5TW. (Tel. 01737 357887).

The CAS archives can be visited by appointment by anyone who has a specific requirement. The contact is Peter Skinner, 32 Mount Felix, Rivermount, Walton-on-Thames, Surrey KT12 2PJ. (Tel. 01763 244619 during the week or 01932 220035 at weekends). If you have any Croydon memorabilia, Peter would be delighted to hear from you. Why not come along to the Airport Visitor Centre in the refurbished Control Tower, open on the first Sunday in each month from 11.00 a.m.–4.00 p.m. – we would be delighted to see you!

Delivered to Railway Air Services on 12 August 1936, D.H.86A G-AEFH *Neptune* was converted to D.H.86B standard the following year by the addition of endplate fins on the tailplane. Normally ten seaters, the '86s had four 205hp D.H. Gipsy Six engines.

One

The First Airport
1915-1928

Growing out of the airfield established in 1915 for the military and used by the Royal Flying Corps, a new civil aerodrome, as it was initially termed, was quite rapidly built up from the old military hangars and buildings, although obviously everything was rather basic but it was not long before companies began to establish themselves, with airlines setting up their own buildings.

There was a ready supply of surplus military aircraft which could be both obtained and converted cheaply for civil use so long as comfort was not the main criterion! Plenty of Avro 504s, Bristol Fighters, D.H.4s and D.H.9s were on the spot and dismantled in the adjoining National Aircraft Factory, while a number were snapped up for the home and export markets, some of which are illustrated on these pages.

However, this glut was bigger than the market could stand, and many of the surplus airframes and engines were eventually scrapped, perhaps for the general good of the aviation industry, since as long as very cheap surplus types were available there would be no demand for new, and therefore more expensive, designs. Indeed it was another decade before new types began to appear in the light aircraft field, while many of the airliners, large and small, were little more than derivatives of military types, although an early manufacturer which began building for the civil airline market was the Dutch company Fokker.

The first terminal buildings and control tower in the early 1920s had little to offer passengers. The tower was particularly basic and was replaced after several years with a taller structure incorporating a new glass top.

More than fifty D.H.6 primary trainers were sold in 1919 from surplus stocks for civil purposes. This example, G-EANU, based at Croydon, belonged to the Leatherhead Motor Co. and had a 90hp Curtiss OX-5 engine instead of the usual RAF 1A. It was withdrawn from use in May 1924.

The Aircraft Disposal Co. was situated in the National Aircraft Factory at Waddon after the end of the war in 1918. Many surplus D.H.4s and '9s were stored awaiting disposal, stacked like this to save space. It is probable that most of these were eventually scrapped.

Airco D.H.9B K-109 was registered on 30 April 1919, a three-seat conversion of H9277. The K-series was a temporary UK civil register and K-109 became G-EAAC on 22 July 1919. Alan Cobham had joined Airco to carry out aerial photography from Croydon and did so successfully for a short time until Airco went into liquidation, its assets being bought by Aerofilms.

Nine de Havilland D.H.16s were built, conversions of surplus D.H.9As with a widened rear fuselage accommodating four passengers in the cabin. All initially served with Aircraft Transport & Travel Ltd, beginning in 1919. Two were lost in crashes and the rest had been withdrawn by 1922. This is G-EAPM *Agincourt* with items being loaded including two spare wheels.

An early scene of the first airport, its name spelt out in massive letters. Visible are Farman Goliath F-FHMU of CGEA and Farman Line, an Avro 504 and a Belgian D.H.4A.

Vickers Vimy Commercial G-EASI *City of London*, delivered to Instone Air Line, flew an inaugural service to Brussels on 9 May 1920, with jockeys as its ten passengers. Powered by 390hp Rolls-Royce Eagle VIII engines, it worked hard over the next four years and, when handed over to Imperial Airways on 1 April 1924, had flown 107,950 miles. It was scrapped in 1926.

A number of Bristol F.2B Fighters were converted in the 1920s for civilian use as three-seaters known as Type 47 Tourers and several were sold abroad. They included five for Spain, and M-AFFF was the last, being ferried out in summer 1921. The engine was a 180hp Wolseley Viper; this photograph is meticulously dated at midday on 26 August 1921, with the c/n given as 6110.

Another remanufactured Bristol Fighter for Spain was M-MRAC, but these differed from the Bristol Tourers in having a 300hp Hispano-Suiza engine. They were ferried out between August 1921 and March 1922, the pilots including several well-known names such as Hereward de Havilland, C.F. Wolley Dod and Frank Courtenay.

The Aircraft Disposal Co. also remanufactured surplus D.H.4s for sale to the Belgian and Spanish air forces and M-MHDO was for the latter. Unlike the civil conversions, the Scarff ring machine-gun mounting was retained in the rear cockpit.

13

Brequet 14T.2 F-ADAI of Cie des Messageries Aériennes (CMA) lurks in front of a Farman Goliath. Powered by a 300hp Renault engine, the Breguet carried two passengers in the cabin with the pilot in an open cockpit above and behind. Total production of the type from 1916 to 1926 reached around 8,000.

In October 1920, M. Lecointe landed at Croydon in his Nieuport 29 F-ICGT while taking part in a Paris-London-Paris race. Five aircraft were involved but only three reached Croydon, the other two being Spad 27 F-CMAY and Potez S.E.A.VII F-FRAA. The two non-arrivals were another Nieuport and Farman Goliath F-GEAD; the weather was said to be very unfavourable.

On show at the 1920 Air Conference were Airco D.H.16 G-EAQS of Aircraft Transport & Travel and BAT FK.26 G-EAPK of Instone. There were nine British-owned D.H.16s and the last three, which included G-EAQS, had a 450hp Napier Lion engine in place of the usual 320hp Rolls-Royce Eagle. It was scrapped at Croydon in 1922. Four of the ungainly FK.26s designed by Koolhoven were built by the British Aerial Transport Co. and 'APK was the last of these four-passenger aircraft; it crashed on 31 July 1922.

Also at the 1920 Air Conference was this line-up. Aircraft Transport & Travel's D.H.18A crashed at Argueil, France, on 13 May 1921, while Instone's famous Vimy Commercial G-EASI was scrapped in 1926. The Westland Limousine beyond is G-EARV, sold to Canada in 1924 as G-CAET, was scrapped there due to wood rot and never achieved Canadian certification. At the end are Avro 547A Triplane G-EAUJ and a Bristol Coupe.

Four versions of the Bristol 47 Tourers, re-worked from Bristol Fighters, were built. Croydon-based S. Instone & Co. Ltd bought G-EART in March 1920 for charter work, carrying two passengers side-by-side in the rear cockpit; the engine was a 240hp Siddelely Puma. This Type 47 had a short life, being withdrawn from use in February 1921.

This Fokker F.II operated the first KLM flight to Croydon using the Dutch airline's own aircraft on 30 September 1920. It wore a complex paint scheme and carried four passengers in the cabin plus one with the pilot in the cockpit. Brand new, it had been registered only seventeen days earlier. Sold to Sabena as O-BAIB in August 1927, after 655 flying hours with KLM, it later became OO-AIB and was broken up in 1937.

One of two Airco D.H.4s supplied to SNETA (Syndicat National pour l'Etude des Transports Aériens), Belgium, was O-BATO with a 375hp Rolls-Royce Eagle engine. Two passengers were carried facing each other in the enclosed cabin. Converted from H5929, it was registered in August 1920 and was destroyed in a hangar fire at Brussels-Evere on 27 September 1921. In the background is a Breguet 14T.

Aircraft Transport & Travel's D.H.9B, G-EAGY, ex-H9258, in the colours of the Compagnie Générale Transaerienne being loaded, or unloaded. Note the three cockpits. This aircraft was sold abroad in January 1921.

Handley Page O/10 G-EATM, ex-D4609, was registered in May 1920. Nine O/10s seating twelve passengers joined three O/7 freighters of Handley Page Transport Ltd, whose services were transferred from Cricklewood to Croydon on 27 May 1921. Powered by two 360hp Rolls-Royce Eagle VIII engines, the O/10s were replaced from 1922 by W.8bs, but G-EATM was wrecked in a gale following a forced landing at Berck-sur-Mer, France, on 29 December 1921.

The starboard 360hp Rolls-Royce Eagle VIII engine of Handley Page W.8b G-EBBH *Prince George* of Handley Page Transport Ltd. It passed to Imperial Airways and was withdrawn from use in April 1929.

The post-war glut of military aircraft included a large number of Avro 504s and many of these were civilianised, being suitable for joy-riding. Some were converted to three-seaters with an 80hp Renault engine and were designated Avro 548, such as G-EAPQ seen here against the backdrop of the original airport buildings. Registered in March 1922, it was written off in October that year.

Avro 504K G-EAIR, ex-E4164, was registered to Aircraft Transport & Travel at Croydon in November 1919, passing to the locally-based Surrey Flying Services twenty-two months later. It was probably used for joy-riding until it crashed at Hayling Island on 21 August 1923.

A long way from home in 1922 was Avro 504K G-EAHY, ex-H7513 and inscribed Wm Beardmore & Co. Ltd, Renfrew Flying School, No.3. Previously owned by the West of Scotland Aviation Co. Ltd, it was one of five purchased by Beardmore to serve a Reserve Training contract and was one of three survivors sold to the North British Aviation Co. Ltd at Hooton for joy-riding; it was withdrawn from use in August 1928.

Air Union's Farman Goliath F-GEAI *Vendée* was taken over from Cie des Grandes Express Aériens when Air Union was formed in 1923. This version, the F.60, had 230hp Salmson 2.9 engines, but most were later upgraded to 260hp Salmsons. Notable is the strange twin-wheel undercarriage. Four of the CGEA Goliaths had registrations including the letters GEA.

An interesting photograph taken from the Airship R36 on Ascot Day, 1921. The view looks east, with Plough Lane at the bottom. Only two aircraft are visible, the light-coloured one appears to be a Breguet 14.

19

Instone Air Line operated four D.H.18s and G-EARO, registered in March 1920, was a veteran by the time this photograph was taken in 1922, judging by the exhaust stains on the registration. It carried eight passengers and by the time it was retired from airline service in 1923 had flown 90,000 miles without mishap. It ended its life on test work at the RAE Farnborough from 1924 to 1926.

A detail view of a D.H.34, possibly one of five used by Daimler Hire Ltd, Croydon. The engine was a 450hp Napier Lion – note the fixed ladder for access to the cockpit over the exhaust, no doubt a perilous journey when leaving when the engine was hot! Perhaps the tray attached to the fuselage was to enable a mechanic to turn the engine with the handle protruding beneath the exhaust.

The prototype Vickers Vulcan G-EBBL with a 360hp Rolls Royce Eagle VIII engine carried eight passengers with one pilot – one wonders why it was so obese, which soon earned it the title of Flying Pig! Instone received 'BBL *City of Antwerp* and two others, 'BDH and 'BEA, in August 1922. This one was scrapped at Croydon in May 1924.

One of two Bleriot 115s used by Air Union on the London-Paris service, F-AGEM had, when this photograph was taken, four 180hp Hispano-Suiza engines. It was later re-engined with 230hp Salmsons and designated Bleriot 135. It had accommodation for ten passengers; a further development was the Bleriot 155.

Bleriot Spad 33 F-ACMA of Cie des Messageries Aériennes and later Air Union having its fuel tank and engine checked – note removal of the cowling and a drape over the open door above the undercarriage. There were forty production aircraft with 230 or 260hp Salmson engines; the enclosed cabin seated four passengers with the two pilots in an open cockpit above and behind.

An attractive painting by Kenneth McDonagh of a Bleriot Spad 33 over the first Croydon Airport. Since only F-ACMA had the oval window and one round window, the artist appears to have made a slight error, as by the shape of the lettering this could be F-ACMH!

The Bleriot Spad 56/4 was a development of the 33, the separate cockpits of the latter being replaced by a wide two-seater beneath the wing leading edge, and there were six passenger seats. The engine was a 420hp Jupiter; the roof windows are interesting.

KLM operated 16 Fokker F.IIIs from 14 April 1921 when G.R. Hinchliffe flew the Croydon-Rotterdam-Amsterdam service and Gordon Olley flew it the other way. H-NABV and 'ABU had the wing mounted on struts above the fuselage and a 360hp Rolls-Royce Eagle engine; 'ABV was sold to Pacific Air Transport, New Guinea, in 1930.

Left: This photograph of a Sopwith Snipe rounding a racing pylon was probably taken at Croydon on the occasion of the first Race Meeting in September 1921.

Below: A line up at the first Croydon Race Meeting in September 1921 shows, from left to right, Airco D.H.6 G-EAWV, one of two S.E.5As (race number 13) and Airco D.H.4 G-EAXC (no.10). There were five events at this meeting, the entries being all ex-military aircraft.

Opposite top: Maj. Wilfred Blake bought D.H.9 H5738 and had it reconditioned at Croydon as G-EBDE for a round the world attempt. The pilot was Capt. Norman Macmillan with Lt-Col. L.L. Broome as photographer. Departing on 24 May 1922, the aircraft was damaged in a forced landing at Istres, Marseilles, and replaced with another D.H.9, G-EBDF, painted as G-EBDE to maintain the deception. The rest of the story is far too long to narrate here.

Farman Goliath F-GEAC originally served with Cie des Grandes Express Aériens and later passed to Air Union, while the antiquated D.H.6 G-EAWV was one of three belonging to the Martin Aviation Co. in the Isle of Wight converted to three-seaters with an 80hp Renault engine. It was withdrawn from use in 1925.

Handley Page Transport Ltd transferred its operating base from Cricklewood in May 1921 but its O/10s experienced difficulty in taking off with a full load. Reductions in the fuel load and removal of wireless equipment and reducing passengers to ten solved this, but by 1922 the O/10s were being replaced by W.8bs. The company operated nine O/10s; G-EATH, ex-D4631, received its C of A in June 1920 and was the last in service, being scrapped at Croydon the following year.

The first race for the King's Cup was held at Croydon on a bitterly cold 8 September 1922, with a twenty-one-aircraft entry, eleven of which completed the course. The winner was Frank Barnard in the Instone Air Line D.H.4A G-EAMU, one of the oldest aircraft in the race.

The Avro 536 G-EAKJ, a variant of the 504, had a fuselage width increased by 9in to accommodate four passengers in the rear cockpit and was powered by a 130hp Clerget engine. This 536 was withdrawn from use in May 1926; the photograph is dated 1922.

The Surrey Flying Services Avro 504K G-EBFW, ex-E1850, gained its C of A on 1 May 1923. It crashed at Mudford, near Yeovil on 17 September 1926. Surrey had a large fleet of 504s and charged 5s for short trips from Croydon. Its last aircraft remained in service until 1934.

Daimler Hire Ltd based at Croydon operated six D.H.34s with 450hp Napier Lion engines and G-EBBS was their second. Certificated in May 1922, it had a short life, crashing near Ivinghoe Beacon, Bucks, on 14 September 1923 with six fatalities.

Instone Air Line was also a D.H.34 operator and its G-EBBT *City of New York* inaugurated the company's Croydon-Brussels service on 7 May 1922. Eight passengers could be carried. When Imperial Airways was formed on 1 April 1924 it inherited six D.H.34s including this one which was converted to a D.H.34b with longer wings in 1925. Eleven D.H.34s were supplied to British operators and one to Dobrolet, Russia.

Seven production Boulton & Paul P.9s were built and G-EASJ was the second. Powered by a 90hp RAF 1A engine, it was bought in April 1922 by Frank Courtney who based it at Croydon. It flew in that year's King's Cup race piloted by C.T. Holmes. In 1928 the Henderson School of Flying took the P.9 to the Cape on a joy-riding tour and it was sold there, becoming G-UAAM, later ZS-AAM.

A number of Armstrong Whitworth Siskin single-seat fighter prototypes were used as civil demonstrators and racers. The Siskin II G-EBEU was a two-seater and took part in the first King's Cup race at Croydon in 1922 flown by Frank Courtney. It was withdrawn from use in November 1924.

First flown in June 1921, the Bristol Type 62 Ten-seater G-EAWY with a 450hp Napier Lion engine was demonstrated to delegates at the Second Imperial Air Conference in February 1922, and in June that year entered service with Instone on their London-Paris route. Later sold to Handley Page Transport, it was used to carry cargo on their London-Cologne freight service. It was withdrawn from use in November 1923.

Part of the interior of the Bristol Ten-seater G-EAWY shows it to have been distinctly spartan, with no luggage racks. Note the clock on the bulkhead with a headset hanging over it.

The seventh Aerial Derby was flown at Croydon on 7 August 1922 and attracted nine entrants, three of which retired. Avro Baby G-EAUM was flown by Bert Hinkler and finished last. After passing through several owners, including F.G. Miles, the Baby was cancelled from the register in December 1934.

Martinsyde F.6 G-EBDK was built as a single-seater for F.P. Raynham and flown by him in the 1922 event, achieving third place in the handicap at 107.85mph. It had a 200hp Wolseley Viper engine and came second in that year's King's Cup race. It was dismantled at Brooklands in April 1930.

Winner of the 1922 Aerial Derby was J.H. James in the blue and white Gloucestershire Mars I G-EAXZ at 177.85mph. It was a one-off single-seater developed from the Nieuport Nighthawk with a 450hp Napier Lion engine. Bought by the Air Ministry in 1923 as J7234, it was later converted to a seaplane trainer for Schneider Trophy pilots and fitted with a 525hp Lion. It was scrapped in November 1922.

Fl. Lt W.H. Longton crosses the finishing line in the 1922 relay race for the Air League Challenge Cup in ADC S.E.5A G-EAXQ, entered by RAF Uxbridge. Winners were RAF Kenley. The S.E.5A was scrapped in November 1922.

First home in the 1922 Aerial Derby was the Mars I G-EAXZ, but Larry Carter in Bristol M.Id G-EAVP came first in the handicap at 107.85mph, here sweeping low over the finishing line. Six of these surplus single-seater fighters became civil in 1919. Powered by a 100hp Bristol Lucifer engine, G-EAVP flew in several races but crashed during the 1933 Grosvenor Challenge Cup near Chertsey, killing the pilot.

Although this photograph was taken at Filton, Bristol, it is of interest as it shows Captain Gordon Olley (with goggles) in Croydon-based Handley Page O/10 G-EATK which he had flown to Filton in winter 1921 to have its 360hp Rolls-Royce Eagle engines replaced by 436hp Bristol Jupiters as shown. No more O/10s were converted and 'ATK was scrapped in August 1922.

Airco D.H.9c G-EBCZ was one of eight belonging to the de Havilland Aeroplane Hire Service, based at Stag Lane. The rear cockpit of the '9c was moved back to accommodate a third passenger; Powered by a 240hp Siddeley Puma engine, 'BCZ was registered in April 1922 but had a short life ending in a crash at Newcastle on 4 July 1923.

The prototype D.H.34 G-EBBQ, in an all-red scheme, was ordered by Daimler Hire Ltd and made its first flight on 26 March 1922, with Alan Cobham as the pilot. Its inaugural flight from Croydon to Paris followed on 2 April. Nine passengers could be carried plus two pilots but the type had a poor record with six of eleven built crashing within two years, 'BBQ being lost at Rotterdam on 27 August 1923.

Developed from the Bristol Type 62, the Type 75 G-EBEV was also a ten-seater including the crew of two, but had a 425hp Bristol Jupiter IV engine. It flew in August 1922 and was shown at the Second Imperial Air Conference in February 1923 as the Bristol Pullman. Converted to the Type 75A Freighter in February 1924, it was leased to Imperial Airways but was withdrawn from use in 1926. Only two others were built.

Delegates at the February 1923 Conference taking an interest in Avro Aldershot J6852 which was demonstrated by Sqn Ldr Roderick Hill. Powered by a 1,000hp Napier Cub engine, the Aldershot last served with the RAE, Farnborough, and was struck off charge in December 1927.

Fl. Lt Hammersley in Avro 552 G-EAPR with a 180hp Wolseley Viper engine crosses the finishing line of the 1923 Aerial Derby, winner on handicap but sixth overall at an average speed of 108.5mph. This aircraft was tested with floats and a number of engines, and the fuselage became the Avro 552A G-ABGO, used for banner towing until it crashed in October 1933 at Coal Aston, Sheffield.

The line up of RAF Bristol Fighters for the Air League Challenge Cup on Bank Holiday 1923. Fifteen RAF stations were represented and crews were given their maps of the 100-mile course one hour before the start. Disastrous navigation meant that only three correctly went round one turning point, while others were so far away that observers could not take their numbers!

Fl. Lt W.H. Longton takes off in G-EAKI labelled Sopwith Hawker, an aircraft which started life as the Sopwith Schneider floatplane, flown by Harry Hawker in the 1919 Schneider Trophy Race which was abandoned due to fog. At the Croydon meeting it averaged 163mph on its 400hp Bristol Jupiter engine and came second overall, seventh on handicap. It crashed at Burgh Hill Golf Course, Surrey, on 1 September 1923.

Alan Butler's black and gold D.H.37 G-EBDO *Sylvia*, with a 275hp Rolls-Royce Falcon engine, had just returned from a competition in Gothenburg to fly in the 1923 Aerial Derby, piloted by Maj. H. Hemming. Starting seventh he was eighth at the end of the first lap but unfortunately had to retire at Romford. The aircraft was destroyed during the Bournemouth races in June 1927.

A group at the 1923 Imperial Air Conference; left to right, a Supermarine Seagull, Avro Aldershot and Vickers Vixen G-EBEC. The latter had a 450hp Napier Lion engine and was later fitted with a longer fuselage; it was withdrawn from use in Febuary 1930.

D.H.9As of No.39 Squadron, Spitalgate, Lincolnshire, preparing to take-off for their fly-past at the 1923 Conference. The second aircraft, E960, was one of a number later rebuilt, becoming J7017. As such it was struck off charge in 11 January 1927 after its undercarriage collapsed on landing.

The Imperial Air Conference on 10 November 1923 involved almost sixty aircraft including the Fairey Flycatcher amphibian N165, the third prototype Flycatcher, which had been shown at the RAF Pageant in June.

A rather ragged D.H.9A formation passes over a Sopwith Snipe at the November 1923 Conference. Snipes served a number of squadrons at home and overseas. The muddy state of the ground at this time of year is apparent.

Alan Cobham prepares to leave Croydon on 16 November 1925 in D.H.50 G-EBFO on a survey flight to Cape Town where he arrived on 17 February 1926. In the cabin with his camera is B.W.G. Emmott acting as photographer. This was the aircraft in which Cobham made several long-distance flights, earning him a knighthood; it ended its days with West Australian Airways as VH-UMC, being withdrawn from use in September 1934.

A typical rural scene at the first airport with Airco D.H.9 G-EBEP and Avro 536 G-EBTF of Surrey Flying Services. The date would be between August 1927 when the 536 was registered and November 1928 when the D.H.9 crashed at West Hill, Sanderstead, Surrey. The 536 was withdrawn from use in December 1930.

Fokker F.II O-BAIB of Sabena, formerly KLM's H-NABD (see page 16), joined the Belgian airline in September 1927 along with O-BAIC, ex-H-NABC. They served for about six years, with 'AIB passing through four private owners before being cancelled in May 1936. In the background is a Handley Page W.8.

The Aircraft Disposal Co. at Croydon assembled four Avro 504Ns from surplus military stocks for Argentina in 1926 – formerly E444, H2512, H2565 and F8841. They had standard 504K wings but 100hp Lucifer engines developed by the Cosmos Engineering Co., later known as the Bristol Lucifer.

Several versions of the Handley Page W.8 were built, G-EBIX being the sole W.8f which had two 240hp Siddeley Puma engines between the wings and a 360hp Rolls-Royce Eagle IX in the nose. Ten W.8es in similar configuration were supplied to Sabena; the W.8f was slightly modified with cabin heating for Imperial Airways. It entered service in November 1924 and could carry twelve passengers, but crashed near Neuchatel, France, on 30 October 1930.

A further development of the Handley Page W series was the W.10, a sixteen-passenger airliner of which four were delivered to Imperial Airways in 1926. Looking very new is the third, G-EBMS *City of London*, which lasted only seven months before crashing in the English Channel on 21 October 1926, a similar fate befalling G-EBMT on 17 June 1929.

Airco D.H.9 H9147 was civilianised as G-EBJX in August 1924 for Northern Air Lines, Manchester, and served with Air Taxis Ltd from March 1927 until it crashed in January 1929. The three-seat configuration can be seen here; the engine was a 300hp ADC Nimbus. Behind is one of Imperial's Handley Page W.10s.

The Czech Avia Co. built a series of two-seat monoplanes in the 1920s-1930s and L-BONB was an Avia BH-11 with a 60hp Walter engine. A number were civil registered while others were supplied to the military as communications aircraft. L-BONB was later re-registered L-BONU; some aircraft were later re-engined with an 85hp Walter.

Two
Between the Wars
1928-1939

When the new terminal was opened in 1928, things were changed considerably for the better, certainly so far as passenger facilities were concerned. In addition to the terminal building, the splendid Aerodrome Hotel was built next to it, providing not only good accommodation but a roof and garden area from which aircraft movements could be watched – truly the beginnings of aircraft spotting in comfort!

For a year or two the older airliners such as the Farman Goliath and Handley Page types soldiered on, but the appearance of the big Handley Page H.P.42 brought a new comfort to flying and, even if it was no faster, it was certainly safer and more reliable.

Other new types began to appear – Fokkers from Holland, Junkers and Focke-Wulfs from Germany, Savoia-Marchettis from Italy, Wibaults from France and then the real air transport breakthrough with the all-metal Douglas DC-2s and 3s. On the lighter side came a mass of de Havilland types from Gipsy, Puss and Leopard Moths to the larger Dragons, Rapides and D.H.86s.

As war clouds gathered in 1939, preparations began to move the Imperial Airways fleet to Whitchurch, near Bristol, and Croydon's airport buildings received camouflage paint. It was to be another six years before normality returned and genuine commercial services could be resumed.

The radio room in Croydon's control tower in the 1930s had a very basic bench and hard chairs – comfort obviously did not count for much in those days!

When the new airport was opened in 1928 a vast improvement in passenger facilities was apparent. The main booking hall featured an island with clocks showing various times in other parts of the world. The departure hall entrance is just visible to the left of the clock tower while on its right is the weather report board showing likely weather on various routes.

The interior of the control tower of the new airport with controllers working out an aircraft's position on the plotting board. Today, the refurbished control tower shows visitors how things were done in those early days.

Passengers were brought from central London to the airport by motor buses operated by the airlines. Here, passengers have either just arrived or are waiting to leave for London. Their baggage was carried on the roof.

Farman Goliath F-AECU *Normandie* of Air Union. Twelve passengers could be carried and a variety of engines from 230 to 260hp could be fitted. The Goliath was the first real French airliner and around sixty were built for a number of airlines.

This April 1935 photograph, looking north, includes the newly delivered Avro 652s G-ACRM and 'CRN, Short L-17 G-ACJK, D.H.86s G-ACVY and 'DUG, Boulton & Paul P.71a G-ACOX, Armstrong Whitworth Argosy G-AAEJ, withdrawn from use the following month and in the Air France hangar a Wibault 280 and what may be a Farman F.300.

A new Marconi radio direction beacon was installed at Croydon by the Air Ministry in 1937 to help guide pilots in bad weather. Four beams radiated from the equipment and pilots were instructed by the control tower which beam to use. A series of dots indicated left of the path, dashes right. When the hum began to fade the aircraft had passed over the airport.

Handley Page H.P.42W G-AAXD *Horatius* on a damp and windy day – note the horizontal windsock and flag above the cockpit. *Horatius* was granted its C of A in April 1930 and was damaged beyond repair in a forced landing at Tiverton, Devon, on 7 November 1939. Imperial Airways operated eight H.P.42s in two versions – the H.P.42Es had 490hp Bristol Jupiter XIF engines, and the H.P.42Ws had 555hp Jupiter XFBMs.

The second of two Short L.17s was G-ACJK *Syrinx*. Seen here with its original 595hp Bristol Jupiter engines, it was later re-engined with 660hp Bristol Pegasus XCs with cowling rings. Carrying thirty-nine passengers, the L.17s were used on the Paris and Brussels routes but their instability was not popular with crews or passengers. *Syrinx* was scrapped at Exeter in 1940.

Lufthansa operated nine Rohrbach Roland Is beginning in 1926 as ten-passenger aircraft and D-1297 *Wasserkuppe*, with an open cockpit, was one of these. A further nine Roland Is were acquired in 1929 while D-1297 subsequently became D-AKIL. Engines were BMWs of 250 or 320hp.

Junkers-G 31 D-1310 with passengers about to enter on the other side. Developed from the G 24, it was larger and heavier with three engines – either Gnome Rhône Jupiters, as here, or Siemens Jupiters or Pratt & Whitney/BMW Hornets. Lufthansa bought seven G 31s and D-1310 was the first, delivered in 1928; it was later re-registered D-ADIN.

A typical Croydon scene of the 1930s with a pair of Handley Page H.P.42s on the tarmac. The time is 12.20, so perhaps the distant aircraft, G-AAXD *Horatius*, is awaiting passengers for Paris. The four H.P.42Ws used on the European routes carried thirty-eight passengers, while the H.P.42Es based in Cairo, carried twenty-four.

Imperial's Armstrong Whitworth Argosy G-AACJ *City of Manchester* runs up on the apron in 1929 while baggage is loaded from a coach. Noticeable are the large aileron servo tabs; 'ACJ was withdrawn from use in 1936. In the background is Lufthansa Junkers-G 24 D-1062 *Sylvanus*, which later became D-AJIF. The G 24 had three engines, mostly Junkers L5s of 280 to 310hp, and accommodated nine passengers with a crew of three.

47

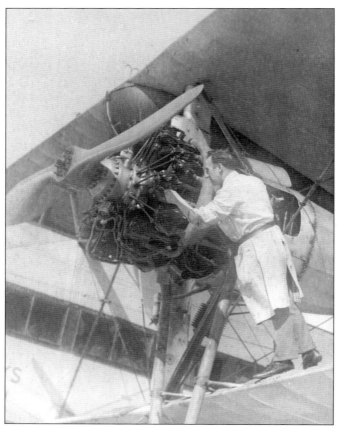

Left: A close-up of the 420hp Armstrong Siddeley Jaguar IVA engine of an Argosy II – the circular section engine nacelle can be compared with that in the Argosy I below.

Below: Servicing Imperial's Argosy G-EBLF with a quartet of ladders. The Argosy seated twenty passengers with the captain and first officer in an open cockpit. Servicing appeared simple, with everything in the open – there is even a mop and bucket man! The Citröen Kegresse half-track (as used in Sahara and Everest expeditions in the 1920s) is interesting.

Developed from the Avro Ten, a licence-built Fokker F.VIIB/3M, the Avro 642 G-ACFV had 460hp Armstrong Siddeley Jaguar VID engines and a cabin holding sixteen passengers. Initially delivered to Midland & Scottish Air Ferries in April 1934, it passed to Commercial Hire Ltd at Croydon and delivered early morning newspapers to the Continent in 1935-1936. It was sold to New Guinea in September 1936 as VH-UXD and was destroyed by the Japanese in 1942.

Four former KLM Fokker F.XIIs were sold to Crilly Airways in 1936, and two to British Airways, G-AEOS and 'EOT. The second was lost in a crash at Gatwick in November 1936, while 'EOS passed to BOAC and was scrapped in June 1940. These two F.XIIs had 500hp Pratt & Whitney Wasp engines and carried sixteen passengers with a crew of two.

Junkers-G 38 D-2000 approaching to land on 1 July 1931; note the four-bladed propellers on the inner engines and two-bladed on the outer engines. At this time it had two 400hp Junkers-L 8 and two 800hp Junkers-L 88 engines and had come from Berlin via Amsterdam. It was re-registered D-AZUR before crashing at Dessau in 1936. For some reason, Croydon's famous smoking chimney has been painted out of the picture, but a trace can be seen just below the undercarriage.

This picture just had to be used, showing the mighty G 38 towering over British Air Transport's Puss Moth G-AAYK – note the long exhaust pipe and wire wheels on the latter. The Puss had a short life; registered on 11 July 1930, it was damaged beyond repair while landing at Heston on 1 April 1932.

Right: A view forward from the rear cabin of the second Junkers-G 38 D-2500. For such a large aircraft, the accommodation seemed rather spartan. Note steps up to the next cabin. Accommodation was provided for thirty-four passengers – two cabins each with eleven seats, a four-seat smoking cabin, three seats in the front of the wing on each side of the fuselage and another two in the extreme nose.

Below: Two Junkers Ju 52/3ms from Sweden were bought in January 1937 by British Airways as freighters, hence the covered windows. Both were shipped to Lagos in November 1940 and were later taken over by Sabena, 'ERU being used for spares and 'ERX becoming OO-CAO, which was withdrawn from use in March 1946.

The all-metal tri-motor Wibault 282 was first used by CIDNA and later by Air France. Total production of the various versions reached eighteen and F-AMHM was the seventh, a 282T.12 with 350hp Gnome Rhône engines. Ten passengers could be carried, but the Wibaults began to be replaced by sixteen-seat Bloch 220s in 1937.

The main interest here is the biplane in the foreground, Nieuport-Delage 391 F-AMDS being loaded from a LEP Transport van. Total production reached thirty-three from 1927; the 391 had a two to three passenger cabin and an open cockpit for the pilot. The engine was a 215hp Armstrong Siddeley Lynx IV and Cie Aérienne Francaise had eighteen aircraft.

Air Union's Liore et Olivier (LeO) 21 F-AIFE in a gold, red and white colour scheme running up with passengers wandering on the tarmac! The first two aircraft were used on the Paris-London route, and the second was re-engined with a 450hp Renaults to become the LeO 212 with a restaurant interior. Twelve passengers could be carried; F-AIFE crashed in fog at Selsdon Park, not far from the airport, on 17 September 1932, killing one person and injuring another.

Croydon in the grip of winter from a H.P.42 cockpit. Nothing is stirring and nothing else is outside the hangars – little chance of getting anywhere that day!

A contrast with the snow scene is this night shot of Armstrong Whitworth Ensign G-ADSS *Egeria*, the second of fourteen built. The first twelve were Mk 1s with 850hp Armstrong Siddeley Tiger IXC engines, as shown here. After 2,686 flying hours, 'DSS was scrapped at Hamble in March 1947.

Above: Fokker built four F.XXIIs, a scaled-down version of the F.XXXVI, with 500hp Pratt & Whitney Wasp engines and accommodation for twenty-two passengers. Three aircraft, PH-AJP to 'AJR, were delivered to KLM between March and May 1935, while a fourth went to Sweden as SE-ABA. PH-AJR became G-AFXR and 'AJP G-AFZP for British American Air Services and Scottish Aviation respectively in 1939, but in October 1941 both were impressed as HM159 and '160. The former was lost after a mid-air fire.

Left: The strange layout of a Fokker F.XXII cockpit where the co-pilot sat behind the pilot whose seat swivelled. The small seat below facing rearwards was presumably for the navigator. The co-pilot had a minimum of instruments but could at least see the compass – the whole arrangement seems extremely crude!

KLM's Fokker F.XXXVI PH-AJA was the only example built. With a crew of four and thirty-two passengers, it was powered by 750hp Wright Cyclone engines and makes an interesting comparison with the smaller F.XXII PH-AJR. The F.XXXVI was sold to Scottish Aviation in 1939 as G-AFZR; it was written off at Prestwick in May 1940.

The Fokker F.XX *Zilvermeeuw* was the company's first commercial aircraft with a retractable undercarriage. With a crew of three, it seated twelve passengers and was delivered to KLM in November 1933. The original three 640hp Wright Cyclone engines were later replaced by 690hp Cyclones. Only one F.XX was built and was used mainly on the London-Amsterdam-Berlin service. It was sold in October 1936 to Air Tropic as F-APEZ but later went to Spain as EC-45-E with LAPE; it crashed in February 1938 in Spain.

Fokker F.VIIs served airlines in large numbers and had three engines of various types in the 200-300hp category. In addition to those built in the Netherlands, others were built under licence in Poland, Italy, Czechoslovakia and Belgium. OO-AIM was one of twenty-eight F.VIIb/3ms built by SABCA for Sabena, which also operated a Dutch and Polish-built example. Sabena F.VIIs had nine passenger seats and a crew of two.

Lufthansa's Focke-Wulf Condor D-AMHC *Nordmark* with a selection of de Havilland biplane twins in the background, plus an Airspeed Courier. This was the fourth pre-production Condor, written off in 1943, date and location unknown.

Focke-Wulf Condor D-ASBK *Holstein* disembarking passengers. The sleek transport had a forward nine-seat smoking cabin while the main cabin could accommodate 17. This is a B Model with 830hp BMW 132H engines. Considerable airport work seems to be going on in the background.

A pair of Air France Bloch 220s, F-AOHB *Gascogne* and 'QNP *Alsace* share the tarmac with Focke-Wulf Condor D-AMHC *Nordmark* in 1938. Air France had sixteen of the sixteen-passenger Blochs, 'OHB was number 2 and 'QNP 16. A baggage cart is being moved towards the former and a pair of steps towards the Condor. In the distance a H.P.42 is being towed across.

Air France Bloch 220 F-AOHF *Saintonge*, a frequent visitor to Croydon, in an embarrassing situation following a belly landing on a basketball pitch, date and location unknown. First man at the scene of an airline incident, as usual, was the man with a paint pot who attempts to paint out the airline's name! Shortly after came the schoolboys – were you one of them?

The most attractive airliner of the 1930s was the de Havilland Albatross. The prototype flew on 20 May 1937, an all-wood cantilever monoplane which had a crew of four and seating for twenty-two passengers. Imperial Airways, later BOAC, operated seven and G-AFDI *Frobisher* was the first of five airliners, the previous two being mail carriers. Note the smart stairway which in tiny letters says 'Service to Paris'.

Another view of Albatross G-AFDI show ing the beautifully faired 525hp D.H. Gipsy Twelve engines and smart undercarriage covers. This aircraft was destroyed in an air raid at Whitchurch, near Bristol, on 20 December 1940. Two more Albatrosses crash-landed, two were scrapped and the two mail carriers were written off while landing at Reykjavik in 1941 and 1942.

The instrument panel of an Albatross seems extremely basic compared to today's jetliners! It does, however, have a gyro-pilot, the top right instrument to the left of the two circular apertures. In the multiplicity of control knobs, the tallest central one is labelled 'Landing Light'.

Sabena was the first operator of the Savoia-Marchetti S.73, receiving five in the summer of 1935. Eighteen passengers and a crew of five were carried, engines were 600hp Gnome Rhône Mistral Majors. Seven more S.73s were built in Belgium by SABCA for Sabena. OO-AGL was used by 271 Squadron, RAF, between 12 and 31 May 1940, it was interned in Algiers by the Vichy government in September 1940 and flown to Rome as MM60514. From then on, the trail goes cold!

A pair of Provincial Airways de Havilland Dragons with spatted undercarriages. On the left is G-ACBW, with 'CKD on the right. The latter was passed to the League of Nations Union, Croydon, in December 1935 and was immediately sold abroad, going to the Ethiopian Red Cross. It crashed on take off and was burnt out at Akaki on 23 March 1936, while 'CBW was impressed in October 1940 as BS816 and was scrapped a year later.

Alpar at Berne bought three D.H. Dragon Rapides including the prototype, CH-287, which later became HB-ARA, then 'APA before being scrapped in 1961. The others were HB-AME and 'AMU, registered in March 1939 and re-registered HB-APE and 'APU in 1948. All three were joy-riding at Zurich in the late 1950s, 'APU was used as spares for 'APE in 1968 and the latter was sold as D-IGUN in 1969.

Three Koolhoven FK.50 eight-passenger light transports were built at Rotterdam in 1935 with 400hp Pratt & Whitney Wasp junior engines. The first two, HB-AMI and 'AMO had a single fin and rudder, while the third, HB-AMA, had twin fins. All three were operated by Alpar from Berne to Paris and Croydon. One, 'AMO, was lost in a crash in September 1937 but the others survived the war and resumed services in 1946, 'AMI being broken up in 1947 and 'AMA going to Liberia where it crashed as EL-ADV in July 1962.

Opposite bottom: Dragon G-ACPY of Olley Air Services outside the Imperial hangar. Registered in April 1934, it served with Blackpool & West Coast Air Services before going to Aer Lingus in May 1936 as EI-ABI. Restored to Olley in March 1938, it was shot down by a German fighter off the Scilly Isles on 3 June 1941. A total of 115 Dragons were built in England and a further eighty-seven in Australia; the engines were 130hp D.H. Gipsy Majors.

Left: The interior of a Fiat G.18V looking forward. The seats appear to be lightweight but reasonably comfortable, although overhead luggage space is somewhat spartan but there appear to be moveable air louvres. Noticeable are the steps over the wing main spar and apparent absence of a door to the cockpit.

Below: Strikingly similar to the DC-2, the Fiat G.18V carried eighteen passengers and a crew of three. Six G.18Vs followed three earlier G.18s and all served with Avio Linee Italiane from 1936. The G.18Vs had 1,000hp Fiat A.80 RC.14 engines and, although the photograph of the last built, I-EURE, is undated, it is probably June 1938 when the type began to serve Croydon.

The only D.H. Fox Moth of Surrey Flying Services was G-ABUT, unusual in having a built-up coaming behind the pilot. It won the 1932 King's Cup race before sale to SFS, a fact noted on the white fuselage trim behind the cabin, and was used for joy-riding until the outbreak of war. On impressment in 1940 it became X9304 but was struck off charge as written off in November 1941.

A group of Surrey Flying Services personnel in front of their Fox Moth G-ABUT. Three names are given on the back of the photograph – Bullmore, Grant and Wood – perhaps a reader can match these to faces and identify the other three?

Designed by J. Bewsher, the A.L.1 side-by-side two-seater was built at Croydon by Surrey Flying Services in 1929 and had a 95hp Salmson A.C.7 engine. Unmarked here, it became G-AALP and flew at Exeter quite often. It is believed to be still in store there.

In 1933, American film makers Martin and Osa Johnson used Sikorsky S-38 NC29V *Osa's Ark* (foreground) and single-engine Sikorsky S-39CS NC52V *Spirit of Africa* (background) to explore northern Kenya and Tanganyika, a two-year 60,000 mile journey. They passed through Croydon, probably on the way out.

Croydon in Colour

1. Built at Croydon in 1931, the Robinson Redwing G-ABNX side-by-side two-seater had a 80hp Armstrong Siddeley Genet engine. Of ten aircraft built, this is the only survivor and is based at Redhill.

2. Probably the oldest, and certainly the largest, relic of the first Croydon Airport is the fuselage of Air Union Farman Goliath F-HMFU, stored for many years at Chalais Meudon, Versailles, but now exhibited in the Musee de l'Air at Le Bourget. It was a frequent visitor to Croydon with other Goliaths in the 1920s.

3. It was quite a surprise to see, on 10 August 1956, this Japanese-registered Beech Twin Bonanza, JA-5022, belonging to a publishing house. It had arrived the previous day and was probably a Model D-50, introduced in 1956 and looking very new.

4. Also at Croydon on 10 August 1956 was Beech Super E-18S F-OAXQ which had arrived from Prestwick the previous day. Whether it had any connection with the Twin Bonanza is not known. Note the highly polished finish and, beneath the nose, Percival Vega Gull G-AHET can just be seen.

5. Twin Bonanza E-50 N565MR of World Wide Helicopters, a visitor on 29 August 1959, awaits its crew outside the terminal with trolley acc attached. Was this perhaps the last Twin Bonanza to visit before the airport closed a month later?

6. Four Percival Provosts for the Sudanese Air Force parked at Croydon on 20 July 1957. Their Arabic numbers one to four were repeated in Roman characters beneath and c/ns were PAC/F/428 to 431. Tops of the wings were painted green.

7. Avro Anson 19 Series 2 VM373 became G-AKUD in March 1948, then reverted to its military marks and served for a time at Boscombe Down before restoration to the civil register in May 1954. It was sold to Liberia in August 1955, becoming EL-ABC at Croydon, where it is seen on 16 August.

8. Smart Consolidated PBY-5A Catalina N5593V was one of several of the amphibians which passed through Croydon. Here, on 30 May 1959, it awaits nose repairs, with Stafford Road houses in the background. It left the airport at closure on 30 September 1959 and was later abandoned in the Gulf of Aqaba.

9. Seen in the late afternoon of 30 July 1958, the Danish S.A.I. KZ X OY-AOL was designed as an artillery observation aircraft and twelve Mk 1s were delivered to the Danish Army, followed by Mk 2s of which this is an example. The engine was a 145hp Continental; OY-AOL was cancelled in December 1981 but it is preserved at the Danish veterans Flying Museum, Stauning.

10. An interesting pairing on 2 May 1959 of Piper Comanche 250 ZS-CKH, which had just landed, and Omnipol L-40 Meta-Sokol OK-NMB which had arrived on 11 April. On 2 June the latter became G-APUE and is still active.

11. Arrow Active G-ABVE, the second of two built, flew in 1932 but was later stored until it was rebuilt with a 145hp Gipsy Major engine for Norman Jones and the Tiger Club in 1958. It was quite new when photographed outside the Rollason hangar on 2 May 1958 with Tiger Moths G-ACDC and 'PRA. It is still a very active Active!

12. Stinson Voyager N97373 became HB-TRE in April 1947 and was at Croydon on 31 July 1957. It later returned to America as N93PD. The camouflaged Dominie in the background wearing ferry marks G-APBJ was former Dutch Air Force V-2, once PH-VNB and originally NR796. It bacame F-OBGE at Croydon in December 1957.

13. Also visiting on 31 July 1957 were Edgar Percival EP 9s G-APCS and 'CT. What they were doing there is not known, but 'CS crashed into Gibraltar Harbour on 24 August 1962 during film-making, while 'CT was sold to Spain as EC-ASO in April 1962.

14. The attractive five-seat Piaggio P.136-L amphibian G-AOFN was imported from Italy in July 1955, where it had been I-RAIA. Powered by two 260hp Lycoming engines driving pusher propellers, it was owned by Aristotle Onassis and based at Monte Carlo. It arrived at Croydon on 10 August 1955 six days after issue of its C of A, but returned to Italy in 1958.

15. Piaggio P.166 G-APVE was registered on 10 June 1959 and was at Croydon on 15 August. Inheriting the gull wing and pusher propellers of the P.136 amphibian, this six to eight-seater had 340hp Lycoming engines and wingtip fuel tanks. Here, the nose cone is removed; this example went to Australia in September 1963 as VH-SMF.

16. Rollason's hangar on 17 March 1956. Newly-converted is Tiger Moth G-AOHY, ex-N6537, Tiger D-EMAX ex-G-ANJF/DE931 had been there since late January, Messenger G-AILL had recently been assembled and Consul G-AJNE had a cowling removed. The distant Proctor was probably G-AHZY.

26. The Le Vier Cosmic Wind racer G-ARUL was an interesting visitor to the 1980 Fly-In. One of three built in 1947-48 by Lockheed engineers in America, it was imported ex-N22C in 1961. Badly damaged later and rebuilt twice, it is, at the time of writing, based at Duxford. The engine is a 85 hp Continental C85.

27. Another racer at the 1980 Fly-In was Percival Mew Gull G-AEXF with a long history dating back to the Schlesinger Race from London (Portsmouth) to Johannesburg in 1936 when it competed as ZS-AHM. Sold in France in 1939, it survived to be restored as G-AEXF post-war, crashed several times but fortunately is flying still.

28. Gipsy Moth G-ABEV takes off on 5 May 1980 bound for Gatwick with mail for Australia, a tiny re-enactment of Amy Johnson's May 1930 flight to Australia in her Gipsy G-AAAH *Jason*. G-ABEV was sold to Switzerland in 1930 as CH-217, later becoming HB-OKI, and was cancelled in 1964. It reappeared in 1977 and was allocated period marks G-ABEV, marks not originally taken up by a Blackburn Bluebird.

29. An interesting and unique visitor to the June 1988 Fly-In was John Fairey's Flycatcher replica 'S1287' (G-BEYB), seen here chocked and with the cockpit covered. After several years of air show appearances it was presented to the Fleet Air Arm Museum, Yeovilton, where it is now exhibited.

30. Side-slipping in to land in June 1988 is Spitfire PR.XI PL983. After wartime phot-reconnaissance work, PL983 became NC74138 with the US Embassy Air Attache based at Hendon and was raced by Lettice Curtis. Displayed statically at Old Warden from 1950 to 1975, it was restored as G-PRXI for Roland Frassinet and flew in July 1984. Following storage and further restoration in 2000, it was destroyed in a crash during an air show at Rouen on 4 June 2001 with the loss of its pilot Martin Sargeant.

31. Exhibited on the airport forecourt, probably during a Wings Week, were Folland Gnat XM693 and Hurricane P2617 (see page 114). The Gnat was retired as instructional airframe 7891M, but is preserved as a gate guardian at the former Folland factory, Hamble, near Southampton.

32. Seen against a threatening sky in June 1988 is Spanish-built CASA C.1-131E Jungmann G-BECW painted to represent Swiss Air Force A-10. Imported in Summer 1976, it was formerly Spanish Air Force E3B-423 and was rebuilt with parts from G-BECY/E3B-459.

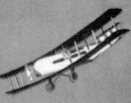

Guide to the Airport of London (Croydon).

IMPERIAL AIRWAYS.

WHSCUDDER.

Amy Mollinson returned to Croydon on 15 May 1936 in Percival Gull Six G-ADZO after a record-breaking flight to and from the Cape, taking seven days, twenty-two hours and forty-five minutes. The Gull had a short life, receiving its C of A on 17 December 1935 and being scrapped after its C of A expired in February 1938 – a sad end for a record breaker.

Percival Vega Gull G-AEEM was registered in May 1936 to Sir Charles Rose, Portsmouth, passing to another private owner at Luton in January 1937, then in November that year to Bowmakers at Luton. Modified to have a 205hp D. H. Gipsy Six II engine, it was sold to Sweden as SE-AHR in May 1939 but was shot down by a German fighter two years later.

D.H.60G Moth G-ABBJ was certificated in June 1930 but seems to have led an uneventful life. Here it appears to have a folded blind flying hood over the rear cockpit. At the time of its impressment in April 1940 as X9303 it was used by Surrey Flying Services. Released to Sound City Films for decoy purposes, it was struck off charge at 20 MU Aston Down on 1 January 1941.

Inscribed 'Rollaston Aviation Co. Passenger Saloon', this postcard shows Desoutter II G-AAZI, an improved version of the Desoutter I, itself a licence-built version of the Dutch Koolhoven F.K.41 being built in the former ADC factory at Croydon. G-AAZI, in a blue scheme, flew in June 1930 and was based at Croydon. It went to Shuttleworth at Old Warden in 1938, was impressed in 1941 as HM507, was dismantled at Twinwood Farm in July 1944 and burnt there the following year.

The eighth Simmonds Spartan was ZK-AAP, built for a solo England-New Zealand flight by H.F. Mase and landing, with enthusiastic onlookers on the roof of the Aerodrome Hotel, at Croydon. Built as a single-seater, it had an eighty gallon fuel tank in the front fuselage.

Spartan ZK-AAP was christened *The All Black* by long-distance flier Lady Bailey at Croydon on 19 April 1929. Leaving Lympne on 26 April, Mase was forced to land in a field in France and crashed there while attempting a take-off.

Four Klemm L.27s were registered in Britain and this is British Air Transport's G-AAWW with a 95hp ADC Cirrus engine. Registered in April 1930, it was based at Croydon where it crashed in February 1933. The L.27 was a three-seater version of the L.26 with an enlarged front cockpit for two passengers.

Surrey Flying Services whose chief engineer F.W.J Grant is shown here, imported Cessna C-34 Airmaster G-AEAI in 1936; it was a four-seater with a 145hp Warner Super Scarab engine. Impressed in 1941 as HM502, it survived to be restored in 1946 but was burnt out at Squires Gate on 20 September 1950.

A foggy day for Lockheed 10A OK-CTB, the second of two owned by the Czech Bata Shoe Co. Originally NC17380, it later went to Canada as CF-BTB then to the RCAF as 7656. After a number of ownership changes, it was last heard of in 1997, flying in its RCAF colours.

The D.H. Hawk Moth was a four-seater built for customers who needed something larger than the two-seater Puss Moth. Eight were completed and two were unfinished; G-AAUZ, the fifth, had a 240hp Armstrong Siddeley Lynx IVA engine and came seventh in the 1930 King's Cup race. Here it is in the colours of Stag Lane-based Air Taxis who acquired it in June 1932. It was sold abroad in December 1938.

Miles Falcon Six G-AEDL and D.H. Dragonfly G-AEEK. The prototype Falcon flew in 1934, but the M.3B Falcon Six had the more powerful 200hp D.H. Gipsy Six engine. Total production of all variants reached around forty and G-AEDL was withdrawn from use in 1939. The Heston-based Dragonfly crashed at Beeding, Sussex, on 17 August 1937 but there were no injuries.

Smart Caudron Aiglon F-ANSB outside the Surrey Flying Services hangar. Two versions were built from 1935, the C.600 with a 100hp Renault Bengali Junior engine and the C.601 with a 143hp Renault 4Pei; this is the former. Around 180 Aiglons were built and F-ANSB was the second. Post-war, F-BDJT appeared with c/n 2, so it may have survived, but other post-war c/ns have appeared as 1, 4 and 5 so there is a possibility of a small batch being built post-war.

Airspeed Envoy G-ADBA of North Eastern Airways runs up outside the company hangar. First flown in June 1934, the Envoy was a six to eight-seater with various engine installations from 185 to 350hp. This example started life with Cobham Air Routes, operated by Olley Air Services, and passed to North Eastern in February 1937. Bought by the Air Ministry in November 1938 as P5778, it joined seven other military Envoys and was used for electrical and wireless instructional purposes.

Lockheed Vega G-ABGK visited Croydon at the end of January 1931. Formerly NC372E it became G-ABFE before being re-registered G-ABGK – an early example of owner Glen Kidston managing to get his initials in the registration. The engine was a 450hp Pratt & Whitney Wasp SC1. Flown to Cape Town in March 1931, it lowered the record to six days and nine hours. Subsequently sold, it took part in the 1934 MacRobertson Race but force-landed at Aleppa. Shipped to Australia, it was rebuilt as VH-UVK.

British Airways imported seven Lockheed 10A Electras in 1937-1938, G-AEPN to 'EPR, 'ESY, 'FCS and 'FEB, all-metal ten passenger transports with 450hp Pratt & Whitney Wasp Junior engines. Here mail is unloaded onto baggage carts on a wet Croydon apron. None of the Electras survived the war; five were lost in accidents, one was destroyed in an air raid at Heston and another was dismantled there.

A scene of some confusion in August 1939 as Imperial's airliner fleet awaits a move to Whitchurch. Visible are Ensigns G-ADSS, 'DST, 'DSW, 'DSX, Albatross, G-AFDJ, H.P.42 G-AAXD and Short Ensign L.17 G-ACJK. Of these, the only post-war survivors were three Ensigns, all scrapped at Hamble while 'DSX was abandoned at Le Bourget in 1940.

The last Lufthansa aircraft to visit Croydon prior to the outbreak of war was Junkers-Ju 52/3m D-AXOS *Oswald Boelcke*, seen from the Aerodrome Hotel on 31 August 1939 about to embark passengers. Just visible over the terminal roof is Ensign G-ADSY. Some new brickwork is evident at the corner of the terminal – perhaps a blast wall in view of the forthcoming conflict.

The one-off Stearman-Hammond Y.150.S. PH-APY was registered to KLM on 25 September 1937 and was demonstrated at Croydon on 10 November. Claimed at that time to be the world's safest aeroplane, it could be landed hands-off. It was acquired in June 1939 by the Royal Aircraft Establishment, Farnborough, as R2676 for tricycle undercarriage trials and was struck off charge on 3 February 1942.

No, its not a Leopard Moth but a Comte AC-12 Moskito, a 1931 three-seater designed by Alfred Comte in Switzerland, who built ten with engines from 95 to 120hp – this one had a 120hp D.H. Gipsy III. First registered as CH-334, these marks were not taken up and it became HB-OLU in May 1934. Based at Lausanne when this picture was taken pre-war, it crashed at Rome in July 1957.

Fokker assembled and sold in Europe thirty-nine Douglas-built DC-2s and PH-ALF for KLM was the thirty-third. Registered in April 1936, it crashed after an in-flight fire at Halle, Belgium, on 28 July 1937 with fifteen fatalities. A plan for Airspeed to build and sell the DC-2 as the A.S.23 did not materialise. DC-2s carried fourteen passengers.

Fokker received the first export Douglas DC-3 and by the outbreak of war had accepted sixty-three of the type for sale in Europe. KLM received a number of Fokker-assembled DC-3s and the first was PH-ALI *Ibis*, seen waiting for passengers to disembark on 6 November 1936 – it had been certificated on 8 October. Leased to BOAC, it became G-AGBB on 25 July 1940, but was shot down on 1 June 1943 by a Junkers Ju 88 over the Atlantic.

Three
Post-War to Closure
1945-1959

As peace returned, so the airport began to adjust to civil flying. The RAF had been operating services with Dakotas but these gradually disappeared to be replaced by other Dakotas in civil colours, all ex-service aircraft now in the liveries of BOAC, KLM, Czech Airlines and others, not forgetting Swissair who were still operating their pre-war DC-2s and 3s, bought new at that time. Air France were using Bloch 220s, slightly smaller than the DC-3.

Post-war momentum in the light aircraft industry was stepped up, but this time surplus military aircraft were mainly Tiger Moths, Magisters and Proctors, with Ansons and Oxfords also available. Other welcome sights were miscellaneous aircraft which had survived wartime impressment to be returned to the civil register. New Austers were coming off the production lines, while Miles were busily turning out Messengers, Geminis and Aerovans and for a while the British light aircraft industry flourished until American Cessna, Beech and Piper imports began to flood in – bad news for the manufacturers over here but welcomed by the spotters! The French aircraft industry was producing a variety of types, many of which visited Croydon, so there was always plenty for visitors to see.

D.H. Dragon Rapide G-AFEP in wartime camouflage with its registration underlined in red, white and blue. Registered in April 1938, it was impressed as X9388 in March 1940 but restored as G-AFEP in November 1940 for Air Commerce Ltd whose title appears beneath the cockpit. Sold to Olley in December 1946, it passed through several owners before sale to Kenya as VP-KFV in June 1948, only to be destroyed by fire in November 1949.

Avro Anson XI PH693 runs up on the apron at 15.37 on 14 August 1945. Passengers appear to be boarding for departure. The Anson was quite new, part of a batch delivered between January and December 1945; it was struck off charge on 15 April 1954.

A mixture of camouflage on ex-RAF D.H. Dominie, built as NR783. It became Dragon Rapide G-AGUG in October 1945 with large civil markings reminiscent of the 1919-1920 period. It went to Pakistan in 1953 as AP-AGL, was restored as G-AGUG three-and-a-half years later but was sold to Dakar in January 1963 as F-OCAG.

BOAC Dakota G-AGFY exhibiting the red, white and blue underlining of registration and fin flash carried during the war and in the early post-war period. Formerly USAAF 42-5636 and RAF FD770, it was sold to South Africa in July 1948 as ZS-DAH. Civil Dakotas could carry up to twenty-eight passengers.

Assembled by Fokker in 1936, this DC-2 became PH-ALE of KLM and was at Lisbon in 1940 when Holland was occupied. Flown to England, it was based at Whitchurch from 1939 to 1945 as G-AGBH. Returned to the Dutch Government as NL203 in February 1946, it was intended to become PH-TBB for KLM but reverted to G-AGBH with Southampton Air Services. It crashed in Malta on 3 October 1946.

Junkers Ju 352A coded GG+YX, surrendered at Eggebek, Germany, was given Air Ministry identification AM19 and made a number of Germany-UK flights between 26 June and 24 August 1945. On 10 August, en route from Farnborough to Fassberg, it became unserviceable and landed at Croydon where it remained until 23 August when it returned to Farnborough. The next day it flew to Schleswig. Ju 352s had 1,200hp BMW-Bramo 323R-2 engines.

Typical of ex-military aircraft being ferried to new homes and wearing hastily applied registrations was Fairchild F-24W Argus HB-EAF. Originally 43-14907, it became HB634 and served with the Air Transport Auxiliary. It was officially (on paper) returned to the USA on 23 October 1946 but was at Croydon the following day! Officially registered in Switzerland in July 1947, it was sold to Germany in April 1956 as D-EDEG.

The RAF was well in evidence in this January 1946 photograph. On the apron is Dakota NL208 of 85 Group Communications Squadron which was struck off charge on 3 September 1947. Landing is another Dakota. Coded DN-U this might have been 512 Squadron. Visible at the extreme right is a RAF Percival Q-6.

Some early post-war services were so hurriedly reinstated that the ex-military Dakotas had not been stripped of their camouflage, although presumably the interiors were more comfortable than the parachutist seats. Here is OO-AUW of Sabena, ex-43-49036, first seen at Croydon by the author in this drab scheme on 25 September 1946. After service in the Belgian Congo, it was sold in July 1973 as N6903.

Swissair was one of the first airlines to re-open services to Croydon post-war. Seen here on 28 May 1946, DC-3 HB-IRA was bought new with HB-IRI in 1937 at a cost of Swiss Fr.527,000. Both DC-3s were sold in January 1955 to Ozark Airlines, St Louis, as N2815D and '2816D respectively.

Swiss DC-3 HB-IRO decants its passengers onto a rather patched apron, with Bristol Freighters G-AGVB and 'HJF behind. The period is probably summer 1946 as G-AHJF was with British American Air Services from August 1946 to March 1947 and was sold abroad in April 1948 as F-BENF, while 'GVB crashed at Le Touquet in November 1958. The DC-3 became N2817D in January 1955.

Originally registered in February 1934, D.H. Leopard Moth G-ACLL was impressed in July 1940 as AW165 and was restored in August 1946 to Rollasons at Croydon where it was photographed on 24 August. It passed to Morton Air Services in November and has since had other owners. It has been in store since 1996.

The prototype Chrislea Ace four-seater flew in September 1946 with a 125hp Lycoming engine and was registered G-AHLG. Production models had a number of changes, including the engine, a 145hp D.H. Gipsy Major 10, and fifteen were completed. A further five were finished but never flown and two more were partially completed. Two Super Aces are currently airworthy in the UK.

A real rarity on 12 September 1946 was French Liore et Olivier LeO 451 F-BCDK, a weather research aircraft festooned with aerials and other protuberances. Built as an attack bomber, it had a speed in excess of 300mph and was powered by a variety of engines from 1,115hp to 1,300hp depending on the variant, of which there were several.

The LeO 451 with another interesting visitor, Noorduyn Norseman OO-AAR, formerly UC-64A 44-70347, on 12 September 1946. Registered in July 1946 to Air Union and based at Knokke-le-Zoute, it was cancelled on 22 June 1950. Designed and built in Canada as a bush-plane, more than 900 Norsemen were produced for the RCAF, USAAF and civilian operators.

A large number of Bücker Bü 181 Bestmanns were registered in France in the early post-war years, ex-Armee de l'Air, and ninety were believed to have been rebuilt by the Brochet Co. This one, visiting on 12 September 1946, had Werknr 331303 and was an ex-Luftwaffe aircraft allocated to No.151 Repair Unit as VN728 on 5 December 1945 and transferred to the Armee de l'Air in April 1946. Here it still wears its RAF fin flash. The engine was a 105hp Hirth HM 504. Post-war production models were built in Sweden and Czechoslovakia.

Siebel Si 204s were used by the Luftwaffe as crew trainers and light transports during the war. Many were built in occupied France at the SNCAC factory where production continued post-war as the Aerocentre NC 701, with an all-glass nose, and the NC 702 with a stepped nose, as here on F-BBFX, visiting on 7 September 1946. Engines were 575hp Argus AS 411s.

Beech Model 17s, known for obvious reasons as Staggerwings, occasionally passed through Croydon and OO-VIT was there on 17 October 1946. With a retractable undercarriage and a speed of more than 200mph, the later versions had a 450hp Pratt & Whitney Wasp Junior engine and, with leather interiors, were truly a gentleman's aerial carriage. OO-VIT, ex-FZ430 and 43-10872, was sold as SE-BRY in April 1950, became HB-UIH in October 1960 and G-BDGK in July 1975. It was cancelled in 1990.

Miles Whitney Straight G-AEWT, registered in May 1937, was sold to France as F-APPZ three months later. The owner's wife flew it to Indo China and back that year, and it was hidden during the war, appearing again at Croydon in August 1946 in dark blue and white. On one visit its tail was damaged by a landing Caudron Goeland. The Whitney Straight was a two-seater with a 130hp D.H. Gipsy Major engine; F-APPZ was destroyed in a fatal crash at St Dizier on 7 July 1954, its home base in 1937.

Several D.H. Dragon Rapides, including TJ-AAA to 'AAE, were supplied to Jordan straight from post-war production, their allocated military serials as Dominies not being used – this batch would have been RL983 onwards. Here, TJ-AAA is being refuelled with, presumably, 'AAB beyond, in September 1946.

The last surviving D.H. Flamingo was G-AFYH of British Air Transport. It had been impressed as BT312 from 7 April 1940 and was restored to the civil register on 24 October 1946. Sadly, it was broken up at Redhill in May 1954. Sixteen Flamingoes were built, later models having 930hp Bristol Perseus XVI engines.

The Royal Aircraft Establishment bought two General Aircraft Monospar S.T.25s for radio development work in 1936, K8307 and '08. The latter survived the war to be registered G-AHBK in February 1946 and visited Croydon on 5 September that year. It was destroyed in a forced landing at Barnsley Wold, near Cirencester, ten months later when it hit the only large tree for miles and was burnt out.

Grumman J4F-2 Widgeon 32943 of the US Navy on a stony hardstanding on 20 October 1946, with a York in the background. Initial production Widgeons had 200hp Ranger engines and Grumman built 276 between June 1940 and January 1949. In 1949-1952 a further forty-one were built in France as the SCAN 30 with 220hp Salmson or Mathis engines.

86

Bristol Freighter 21 G-AHJG was completed as a Mk IIA in 1947 and flown as ZS-BOM by Suidar International Airways between Croydon and Johannesburg. Seen at Croydon on 2 July 1947, named *Golden City* with blue and red trim, it had been damaged in a heavy landing in mid-June. It was subsequently sold to Shell, Ecuador, as HC-SBU in August 1948 but was destroyed in a crash on 6 August 1949 at Salasaca, Ecuador, with thirty-five fatalities.

Several de Havilland D.H.86Bs survived the war to re-emerge at Croydon. This example, SU-ABV, was one of two operated by Misr Airlines, Egypt, in 1937, and was registered as G-AJNB to Peacock Air Charter, Alexandria, in 1947. Why it did not remain on the Egyptian register is not clear, but as 'JNB it was derelict at Wadi Halfa in 1949.

This Anson I, serial 212, was the first of twelve for Portugal's Aeronautica Militar, supplied in June and July 1947, and was formerly NK437. It left Croydon on 21 August 1947 for the liaison and transport squadron at Portela.

Anson I DJ165 became VH-AKI in March 1947 and left Australia on a ferry flight to Croydon for sale, where it was photographed on 27 April with two other Australian Ansons, VH-ALX (DG696) and VH-ALY (AX261). All became British registered, 'AKI becoming G-AJSD; it was scrapped at Southend in 1949.

Sivewright Airways was formed in June 1946 and operated several types including three Avro 19s; G-AIXE was delivered in March 1947 so was quite new when photographed on 24 June. It was wrecked in a forced landing at Chelford, Cheshire, on 7 January 1948.

Belgian airline Sabena bought three de Havilland Doves for service in the Congo and OO-AWE, the thirteenth Dove off the production line, is shown taxiing out at Croydon on 11 October 1947. With 330hp D.H. Gipsy Queen engines, the Dove could carry up to eleven passengers and the type was frequently seen at Croydon where several were based.

BOAC Dakota G-AGFX whooshes past the photographer on a very low approach to set down on a wet apron. Originally USAAF 42-5635, it became FD769 officially but probably did not take up these marks before becoming G-AGFX, then ZS-DAI, then G-AGFX again before sale as ZS-DCZ in June 1949.

In a rather more sedate photograph is BOAC Dakota G-AGKK in polished metal. Originally 43-48839, it passed to the RAF as KJ929 and was registered G-AGKK on 7 November 1944. In April 1949 it was sold as F-OAFQ.

Among the many Dakotas which visited Croydon around 1947 was D-23 of the Czech Air Force. Formerly 43-15114, it was one of twelve used by the military and was later sold to Poland.

Sobelair's Dakota OO-SBB, seen on 9 January 1947 in scruffy wartime colours, was formerly KG550 and originally 42-93153. It had last served with No.525 Squadron at Abingdon and was sold to Canada as CF-ILZ in November 1955.

Dakota OK-WDL of Czechoslovak Airlines on 2 January 1947 showing signs of its USAAF service as 42-92880. It entered service in November 1946 on the Prague-Stockholm route.

KLM Dakotas were frequent visitors from 1946 and PH-TBP shows the Dutch airline's attractive silver and blue colour scheme. A post-war conversion from USAAF C-47A 42-24042, it was registered in June 1946. *The Flying Dutchman* titling was painted on the other side as *De Vliegende Hollander*.

Contrasting with the drab OO-AUW on page 79, Sabena's Dakota OO-AUX had been stripped of its camouflage and previous identity as 42-23800 and rebuilt by summer 1947. It served for a time in the Congo and was sold to Delta Air Transport in 1969. After damage sustained at Amsterdam it was withdrawn from use in 1970, returned to Antwerp and broken up in 1972.

Transair operated a number of Dakotas from Croydon and converted others for customers; this postcard of G-ANEG was given to passengers. The aircraft, originally 44-77112, was leased out with various marks including OD-AEP, 5B-CAY, N26AA and 9M-AUJ but was derelict at Bahrain as G-ANEG when cancelled in 1982.

Thirteen Lockheed 12As were imported and G-AGDT was the eighth, registered in September 1942 to Cunliffe-Owen Aircraft at Eastleigh with B Conditions marks Y-0233. Impressed as HM573, it was restored as G-AGDT in 1946 to Southampton Air Services, as seen here at Croydon on 18 May 1947. It was sold to Sweden as SE-BTO in May 1951.

The Stinson 108 was a post-war development of the 1940 Voyager, a four-seater available in several versions. HB-TRI was a Model 108-2 introduced in 1947 with a 165hp Franklin engine. Registered in July that year, it was previously N9707K; it crashed in the Furka Pass on 18 May 1958. Total production of the 108 series reached 5,260.

Miles Gemini G-AKHB in light blue with dark blue trim, shares the hard standing with Anson VR-TAT, formerly G-AIFA, probably in October 1948. The Gemini was withdrawn from use at White Waltham in April 1965 while the Anson, operated by United Air Services, crashed at Dar-es-Salaam, Tanganyika, on 3 January 1950.

The two-seat Globe Swift with a 125hp Continental C-125 engine was imported by Helliwells of Walsall with the intention of building it, but the scheme fell through. G-AHWH arrived in March 1947 and appears to be attracting some interest here. It was withdrawn from use in June 1961 at Wombleton.

Locally-based St Christopher Travel-Ways operated Dragon Rapide G-AIYP and this Vega Gull, G-AIIT, in summer 1947. The attractive colour scheme was metallic light blue with black registration outlined in white. The Gull, originally G-AFAU, had been impressed as X9332 but for some reason was not restored to its former marks. Sadly, it was withdrawn from use at Croydon in November 1947.

Percival Q-6 G-AHTB was formerly P5634, one of a batch built for the RAF which also received some impressed examples. Granted its C of A on 25 April 1947 with the London & Oxford Steel Co., G-AHTB passed to a private owner at Southend five months later and was damaged beyond repair at Almaza, Cairo, on 2 November 1947.

A smart Percival Q-6 of Cartwright Hamilton Aviation, G-AEYE was the prototype, first flown at Luton on 14 September 1937. Powered by 205hp D.H. Gipsy Six engines, it could carry a pilot and five to six passengers. Twenty-six production aircraft were built and 'EYE was impressed as X9328, serving with several RAF units before post-war restoration in May 1946. It was withdrawn from use three years later.

Converted from Dominie R9564 to a Dragon Rapide G-AKOB, this aircraft was granted its C of A on 19 March 1948 and is seen landing at Croydon five days later. It was sold to Kenya in December 1955 as VP-KNS.

An early post-war product of the Czech Benes-Mraz Co. was the Sokol M.1C, a three-seater with a 105hp Walter Minor engine. OO-AAZ was registered in January 1947 to Air Union at Knokke-le-Zoute and was damaged beyond repair on 18 July 1951. The photograph dates from 1947 or 1948 as Dakota G-AJAZ in the background was sold to Spain in December 1948.

The Praga E.114 Baby two-seater originated in Czechoslovakia in 1934 and licence-production in England totalled around thirty. Post-war production resumed in its home country and 110 had been built when manufacture stopped in 1948. Two versions were built, the E.114D with a 75hp Praga D engine (illustrated) and the E.114M with a 65hp Walter Mikron.

The first Auster J-2 Arrow G-AICA was shown at the September 1946 SBAC Display at Radlett; at that time only British aircraft with British engines could be exhibited but its 75hp Continental was apparently overlooked! The date of this photograph at Croydon is not known, but it was sold to France as F-BAVS in October 1950.

The hangars still showed signs of wartime camouflage when Lockheed Lodestar ZS-BAJ visited Croydon in October 1946. Originally delivered to the US Coast Guard in May 1940, it became ZS-BAJ in 1946 and later passed through a number of US owners, the last known being Florida Air Cargo in July 1967.

Scruffy Anson I EG435 wearing rough ferry marks G-ALEN was one of a number of ex-RAF Ansons sold off post-war. This one was sold in October 1948 but never achieved further civil status, being scrapped three months later.

Republic Seabee amphibian G-AJVO gained its C of A on 15 April 1947. Owned by the Air Transport Association, Guernsey, it passed to a Redhill owner in 1948 but had just been sold to Norway as LN-TSN when it was photographed at Croydon on 14 May 1949. With four seats, the Seabee was somewhat underpowered with its 215hp Franklin engine. Originally NC87654, it crashed on 23 August 1955.

Although allocated ferry marks G-ALOG, Miles Magister BB666 should have been restored to its pre-war marks G-AFXA, but was not reconverted. Seen at Croydon on 12 September 1949, the registration G-ALOG was reallocated to another Magister, L8276.

Three examples of the French SNCASE SE.2300 were built, the first a two-seater with tailwheel undercarriage, while the second and third, respectively two and three-seaters, had tricycles. Further development was abandoned in favour of the Nord Norecrin. F-BEEL, the third aircraft, designated SE.2310, visited Croydon on 2 September 1949.

A number of early Beech Bonanzas, crated to the UK, were assembled at or passed through Croydon from mid-1947 and among them was NC2827V in natural metal finish with red trim on 25 June 1949; it was later resprayed cream and red. What happened to it is not known, but the burnt out wreckage was in the accident hangar at Croydon on 6 March 1954.

Many surplus ex-US military Piper Cubs came onto the European civil registers in the early post-war years and France probably had more than any other country. Visiting on 25 August 1950 was the yellow and red F-BFFD, interestingly an O-59A Grasshopper rather than the much more common L-4 versions.

Beech C-18S G-ALJJ at Croydon on 15 April 1950 had been seen there a year before as VR-HED. Before that it was PI-C80 and originally USAAF 44-87209 with the designation C-45F. Registered in the UK on 2 January 1950, it was sold in May 1952 as VH-KFD.

Airspeed Oxford SE-BTP named *Prince Canasta* and finished in black and orange on 20 June 1951. Originally V3325, it went to the Norwegian Air Force as V-AW before sale to Sweden, later going to Finland as OH-OXA, then OH-VKT, before cancellation in November 1957.

Converted from Oxford DF522 to Consul G-AJNG in June 1947 for Westminster Airways, Blackbushe, this aircraft changed hands twice before sale to Aero Nord AB, Sweden, as SE-BUP in March 1952, with silver wings and blue fuselage. When this photograph was taken on 24 August 1952 it had become silver with blue trim.

Consuls of many nationalities were a common sight at Croydon in the 1950s – on one visit I counted twenty-eight! This example, F-OAFD, was converted from Oxford AT760 in 1947 by Airspeed as G-AJWO and was sold to a Croydon owner in August that year. A year later it went to Tangier as F-OAFD and visited Croydon on 24 August 1952.

Dragon Rapide F-BEFU, ex-G-AJKE, in a colourful blue, white and orange scheme advertised the French drink BYRRH above and below the wings. No date is quoted, but I saw it at Croydon on 16 May 1952.

Croydon did not get many Persian visitors, so smart maroon and white Cessna 195 EP-ACP was welcome in November 1952. By 18 January 1953 it had been resprayed metallic blue and white as seen here, while by 6 June it had become F-BGQJ. In the background is pre-war Taylorcraft A G-AFJP which crashed in October 1953.

Winnie, the red and cream Bellanca Cruisair ZS-DEN (and former CF-GLM) was a visitor on 24 May 1952. It was inscribed 'Dr J.N. Haldeman, Chiropractor, Regina, Sasketchawan'. Various models of the Cruisair were built from the mid-1940s with engines from 150 to 230hp.

Bought as X1050 in 1940 for experimental use by the Royal Aircraft Establishment, Farnborough, this Stinson Voyager was civilianised as G-AGZW in 1946 and in April 1953 passed to a Croydon owner, being sold two months later to Sweden as SE-BYI. A two-seater, the Voyager had a 80hp Continental A80 engine.

Blue and cream Klemm Kl 35D SE-BHE was a visitor on 14 September 1953. The type was built under licence for the Swedish Air Force and when these were retired they came onto the civil market. Powered by a 105hp Hirth engine, it was designated Sk15 in Swedish service.

Lockheed Lodestar N9974, formerly OO-EDS, was a visitor in May 1952 in natural metal finish with red and black trim. It was actually registered N9974F and was delivered via Prestwick to the USA on 1 July 1952, becoming N318. In 1961 it was sold to Mexico as XB-JUP, returning to the USA ten years later.

Two early Beech Bonanzas, HB-ECR and ZS-BPW, share the tarmac outside D hangar with Beech D-17s N18777 on 5 September 1954. Introduced in 1947, early Bonanzas had a 196hp Continental engine; by 1977 production had reached 10,000 and late models had a 285hp Lycoming.

Typical of the ex-military Dominies which passed through Croydon as Dragon Rapides was F-OAPS, originally X7521 and civilianised as G-ALOV in April 1949. The writer saw it as F-OAPS on 27 February 1954 and noted the colour scheme as silver and brown – it had been seen six weeks earlier as G-ALOV in silver and black, belonging to Short Bros.

The Beech Model 17 first flew in November 1932 with a fixed undercarriage, with a retractable model flying in February 1934. Many versions for civil and military customers followed and N18777 was a yellow and black D-17S, introduced in 1937 with a 450hp Pratt & Whitney R-985 engine. Named *Tatu*, it travelled extensively and was at Croydon on 5 September 1954.

Opposite top: An example of the many ex-RAF Tiger Moths parked outside at Croydon for several months in 1954. Taken in March that year, in the immediate foreground is BB748/ G-ADIB which left on 8 June as F-BGZU, T6463/G-ANMR left on 29 May as F-BGZN and T6771/G-ANMT left on the same day as F-BGZO. Tigers converted by Rollason were well finished, but some others seemed to get a quick respray and new marks before flying away!

Opposite below: Looking the other way in the Tiger line, immediate foreground is T7289/ G-ANKF, sold as F-BHIE from Thruxton, N5474/G-ANKZ was not sold until February 1960 as I-LUNI, N6911/G-ANKB stayed even longer, eventually going to Canada in March 1972 as CF-CJW and T6179/G-ANKE left in October 1955 as F-BHIP. It should perhaps be explained that work on the Tigers continued for some time after Croydon had closed, the aircraft being roaded out to fly from somewhere else, sometimes Redhill.

Oops! Miles Aerovan IV G-AILM had passed through several owners since its appearance in 1947 including Silver City Airways at Blackbushe, Aero Publicity at Elstree and Space Neon at Croydon. It was used by the latter for aerial advertising with a framework of neon lighting, but had suffered a nosewheel collapse when photographed on Boxing Day 1954. It was repaired and sold to Greece as SX-BDA in June 1955.

White and blue Piper Pacer 135 ZS-DKA receives attentions to its engine on 9 October 1954. The Pacer, a four-seat development of the two-seat Vagabond, appeared in 1950 with 115, 125 or 135hp Lycoming engines. Production ended in 1954 after 1,120 had been built, to be followed by almost 9,500 four-seat Tri Pacers and two-seat Colts, basically tricycle undercarriage Pacers. Now the wheel has gone full circle, with some Tri Pacers being converted to tailwheel undercarriages.

Entering service with British European Airways in October 1946, Vickers Viking 1A G-AHOW was later with Airwork in 1953 on trooping flights as XD636. Sold to Trek Airways as ZK-DKI in October 1954, it was at Croydon on 7 June 1955 before restoration as G-AHOW. It was withdrawn from use at Manston in September 1967. Viking 1As accommodated twenty-one passengers and had 1,690hp Bristol Hercules engines.

In addition to operating its own Dakotas, Transair converted and serviced them for other operators. Here, F-OAPH waits for attention outside the Transair hangar. Originally 42-92304, it became FZ555, then South African Air Force 6866, then ZS-DCA. Seen at Blackbushe in March 1954 with F-OAPH on the fuselage and G-ANNT on the fin, it was at Croydon a year later, as seen here, and reverted to ZS-DCA.

One of a batch of eleven Miles Magisters registered in February 1949, most of which were scrapped unconverted, N3926 had served with No.24 Elementary Flying Training School. Post-war it became G-ALOE but, fitted with a canopy, was sold to Belgium as OO-ACH. It visited Croydon in March 1955 with another Magister, OO-NIC.

Supplied new to Holland in May 1954, Benes-Mraz Sokol M.1D PH-NFK passed through several owners before the final indignity of being sent in 1968 to a children's playground in Haastrecht. It was later broken up. The author saw it at Croydon on 8 September 1955 in a gold and red scheme, perhaps when this photograph was taken. Compare with the Belgian M.1C on page 97.

Mosquito PR.35 VP200 with rough Canadian ferry registration CF-IMB was at Croydon on 15 August 1955, one of fifteen acquired by Spartan Air Services for high-altitude photo surveys. This and CF-IMA, C, D and E were cannibalised at Bournemouth-Hurn to provide spares for the other ten.

Burmese Air Force Percival Provost T.53s UB201 to 206 overflew London on 25 October 1956 en route from Luton on their delivery flight and stayed overnight at Croydon. The c/ns, in serial order, were PAC/F/180, 200, 211, 212, 231 and 232. Three more, UB213 to 215, c/ns 425 to 427 passed through on 13 October 1957.

The RAF disposed of 254 Percival Prentices for proposed civil conversion between 1955 and 1958 but VR238, at Croydon on 19 May 1956, was not one of them. It had served with Nos 3 and 4 Flying Training Schools at South Cerney and Middleton St George respectively, and here wears the code N-H of the former. It was sold for scrap in June 1957.

Hurricane P2617 and Gnat XM693 (see colour photograph no.31) were exhibited on the airport forecourt, probably during a Wings Week, but the date is not recorded. If the serial is correct, this is the Hurricane in the Battle of Britain Hall at the RAF Museum, Hendon, now coded AF-F of 607 Squadron with which it served during the Battle.

Tiger Moth G-AKXG was converted from T6105 at Croydon to become a single-seat crop sprayer with a hopper beneath the fuselage. This and G-AKXH, in a grey finish and dismantled, were both at Croydon on 31 December 1948; they went abroad respectively as VH-KYA in October 1957 and ZK-AVB in September 1950.

One of a number of post-war conversions of Auster Is for civilian owners, Taylorcraft Plus D G-AHHX was ex-LB314 and was registered in July 1946. Here in the colours of the Croydon Flying Club, it was sold to Germany in 1957 as D-ELUS and later became D-ELUV.

Vickers Viking 1A G-AHPA served briefly with British European Airways for several months before going to the Ministry of Supply as VW217, one of several bought by the Ministry for trials prior to their purchase of the military derivative, the Valetta. Following disposal, it appeared at Croydon shorn of markings except for the registration on the tail, on 17 May 1956. It was scrapped at Wymeswold in 1958.

Czech Air Force visitors to Croydon post-war included not only Dakotas but Junkers-Ju 52/3ms, represented here by D-7. It is known that Czechoslovakia received three former German '52s after the war, so this is presumably one of them. From memory, the colour was dark olive green overall.

Several Beech 18 light transports were operated by the Le Bourget-based Escadrille Mercure in a silver and red scheme, and F-BEDY was a Model C-18S, a wartime production aircraft with the designation C-45, of which more than 5,200 were built with 450hp Pratt & Whitney R-985 engines.

This attractive six-seat twin is the Macchi MB.320 F-BBIM with 185hp Continental E-185 engines. A few were built in 1951-1952, mostly delivered to East Africa. A production agreement for manufacture in France by SFCA as the VEMA-51 came to nothing.

Cessna Bobcat F-BHDJ at Croydon on 14 June 1956 had been sprayed silver but its USAAF serial 42-58484 showed through on the tail. A trainer and light transport, the Bobcat could carry a pilot and four passengers on its 245hp Jacobs R-755 engines. More than 5,400 were built in various versions.

Shell's de Havilland Heron II G-ANUO was a frequent Croydon visitor; as a mini airliner seventeen passengers could be carried plus two pilots. It changed ownership in April 1971 after sixteen years with Shell and was derelict at Biggin Hill for several years before being rescued by the Westmead Group, resprayed by Acebell Aviation and placed outside the airport terminal painted as Morton's G-AOXL which operated the last commercial flight out of Croydon on 30 September 1959. The real G-AOXL was a Series Ib with a fixed undercarriage, whereas G-ANUO's gear was retractable.

A very unusual visitor, date unrecorded, was Fairey Firefly T.7 WJ187. The AS.7 entered service in small numbers, production being concentrated on the T.7 for training observer/radio operators. WJ187 bears the fin code GN, signifying its base to be HMS *Gannet*, Eglinton.

The Noorduyn Norseman, designed for bush operations in Canada, was never common in Europe but another is illustrated on page 82. This one, I-AIAK, was from Italy, date unknown. The prototype Norseman flew in November 1935 and various versions were built with engines from 420 to 550hp.

Another type which was not common in Europe before the war was the Luscombe Silvaire, although these days a number are registered on this side of the Atlantic. On 31 July 1957 SE-AZU shared the parking space outside the toilets with Aerovan G-AJKP.

The Nord 1000 series were post-war production models of the Messerschmitt Bf 108, built in occupied France from 1942. The Nord 1002 had a 233hp Renault 6Q engine and was a four-seater supplied to the French military and civilian owners as shown here by F-BAUC, production aircraft No.158.

The three-seat de Havilland Leopard Moth was a successor to the two-seat Puss Moth and flew in May 1933. With a 130hp D.H. Gipsy Major engine, more than 130 were built, of which sixty were for overseas customers. HB-XAM was supplied new to Switzerland in July 1936 and was not withdrawn from use until August 1960. This photograph is undated but the Consul G-AIOT was withdrawn in August 1955.

Originally registered as EI-ADM in December 1947, this Miles Gemini was bought by *Flight* magazine in mid-1949 and given the appropriate out of sequence registration G-AFLT. It crashed at Burpham, near Guildford, on 10 January 1954.

Piaggio P.136L I-GULL visited Croydon in March 1958, the same year in which another P.136, G-AOFN, returned to Italy. A photograph of the latter appears in the colour section. Total production amounted to sixty-five, including thirty-three for the Italian Air Force.

Airspeed Consul G-AJXI was one of three owned by the Ministry of Civil Aviation Flying Unit for some years from 1947. Converted from Oxford V4283, it was at Croydon on 12 January 1957 as F-BHVY, its Consul-type pointed nose replaced by an Oxford nose for survey work in French West Africa.

Dakota F-OAID of Aerotec, a visitor on 27 April 1957, was originally 42-92603, then KG392, and went to Denmark as OY-AAB, later OY-KLA before taking up its F-O marks. It served with the French High Commission in Cameroon before sale to Airnautic in 1962 as F-BIID and was sold in August 1968 as TR-LML. Nothing more has come to light.

Two Luftwaffe Dakotas visited on 20 October 1957; GA+111 was originally 44-77220, then RAF KP250 and was later sold as N90904. Illustrated is GA+112, ex-44-76692 and KN499 which on retirement from the Luftwaffe became N90905. The Luftwaffe had received twenty Dakotas from 1956.

An unusual military arrival on 22 April 1957 was this de Havilland Canada US Army L-20 Beaver 16808. The Army bought a total of 654 Beavers, the largest fixed-wing post-war order at that time. Later in their life the Beavers were designated U-6A and B.

Another US Army visitor, on 26 July 1957, was Sikorsky H-34 Choctaw 54-3022. Powered by a 1,525hp Wright R-1820 engine, the type bore the Sikorsky designation S-58 and served in large numbers with civil and military operators. In the UK, Westland developed it as the turbine-powered Wessex. Lurking in the background is Aerovan G-AJKP, lost in a fatal crash in December 1957.

Reid & Sigrist Desford G-AGOS flew on 9 July 1945 as a two-seat trainer with 130hp D.H. Gipsy Major 1 engines, later replaced with 145hp Major 10s. It was subsequently modified to have an extended glass nose for prone pilot trials at RAE Farnborough and serialled VZ728. Later used by Film Aviation Services for photographic work, it visited Croydon on 30 July 1958 and is now preserved as VZ728 at Snibston Discovery Park, Coalville, Leicester.

An apparently sad sight on 4 May 1957 was the single-seat Watkinson Dingbat G-AFJA, built in 1938 and flown at Heston in June that year by Ranald Porteus, later to become well-known as the Auster demonstration pilot. The Dingbat had a 30hp Carden Ford engine and was rebuilt at North Weald in 1959. It was last heard of in store near Coventry.

A pair of skywriting North American Harvards visited Croydon in summer 1958. Originally registered D-IDOK and 'GAL, they were re-registered D-FDOK and 'GAL. German registration sequences are based on aircraft weight and the Harvards had obviously been lighter than at first assumed or possibly were lighter with the skywriting equipment removed.

A German arrival in August 1958 was the RFB RW-3 Multoplan D-EFUP, a tandem two-seater with a 75hp Porsche engine in the centre fuselage driving a propeller fitted between the fin and rudder. This example had extended wings and underwing fuel tanks. Twenty-four were built by Rhein Flugzeugbau.

A poor quality print of a very unusual visitor, Malev (Hungarian Air Transport) Ilyushin Il-14P HA-MAI in early October 1958. Around eighty Il-14Ps were built by VEB at Dresden between 1956 and 1958; passenger accommodation was eighteen to twenty-six and engines were 1,900hp Shvetsov Ash-82T-7s. It seems likely that this was the largest tricycle undercarrige airliner to visit Croydon.

Omnipol marketed this agricultural version of the Czech L-60 Brigadyr as the Agricolta and exhibited it at the Paris Air Show in June 1959. It subsequently visited Croydon, presumably for demonstrations. Some 400 L-60s were built, including a four-seat general purpose version, all with 220hp Praga Doris M.208B engines.

A fairly late visitor was Jodel D.112 HB-SUU on 4 April 1959. It was just a year old then but was still current forty-two years later! Since the first single-seat Jodel flew in 1948, hundreds have been both factory and amateur built in many versions.

A familiar sight in April 1957 in the Rollason hangar with Tiger Moth fuselages awaiting attention. Identifiable here are T6903/G-ANMU, sold as D-ECOR in August that year, DE206 and N6476 which became respectively G-APAW and 'PAX. The former crashed at Redhill on 20 December 1959, while 'PAX became HB-UBF in July 1957.

Brand new Rollason-built Turbulent G-APNZ on 22 June 1959, three days before its special category C of A was awarded. The following year it won the King's Cup race at Baginton, Coventry. It was last reported on rebuild after a crash in September 1995. Rollason built twenty of the Druine-designed Turbulents. Note the Tiger Moth fuselages awaiting conversion.

Rollasons built a non-flying Druine Turbulent for static show purposes which hung from their hangar roof when not required. It is seen here on 15 November 1958.